JESSE JAMES

Motorcycle Mania 3

TEXT BY CURTIS CUMMINGS

PHOTOGRAPHS BY ERIC HAMEISTER, JESSE JAMES, AND FRANK OCKENFELS

VIKING STUDIO

Special thanx to everyone who helped make West Coast Choppers what it is

✠

VIKING STUDIO ✠ Published by the Penguin Group ✠ Penguin Group (USA) Inc., 375 Hudson Street, New York, New York 10014, U.S.A. ✠ Penguin Group (Canada), 10 Alcorn Avenue, Toronto, Ontario, Canada M4V 3B2 (a division of Pearson Penguin Canada Inc.) ✠ Penguin Books Ltd, 80 Strand, London WC2R 0RL, England ✠ Penguin Ireland, 25 St. Stephen's Green, Dublin 2, Ireland (a division of Penguin Books Ltd) ✠ Penguin Books Australia Ltd, 250 Camberwell Road, Camberwell, Victoria 3124, Australia (a division of Pearson Australia Group Pty Ltd) ✠ Penguin Books India Pvt Ltd, 11 Community Centre, Panchsheel Park, New Delhi – 110 017, India ✠ Penguin Group (NZ), Cnr Airborne and Rosedale Roads, Albany, Auckland, New Zealand (a division of Pearson New Zealand Ltd) ✠ Penguin Books (South Africa) (Pty) Ltd, 24 Sturdee Avenue, Rosebank, Johannesburg 2196, South Africa ✠ Penguin Books Ltd, Registered Offices: 80 Strand, London WC2R 0RL, England ✠ First published in 2004 by Viking Studio, a member of Penguin Group (USA) Inc. ✠ Text copyright © Payupsucker, Inc., 2004 ✠ Photographs copyright © Eric Hameister, 2004 ✠ Photographs copyright © Frank Ockenfels, 2004 ✠ All rights reserved ✠ CIP data available ✠ ISBN 0-670-03400-2 ✠ Printed in Mexico ✠ Without limiting the rights under copyright reserved above, no part of this publication may be reproduced, stored in or introduced into a retrieval system, or transmitted, in any form or by any means (electronic, mechanical, photocopying, recording or otherwise), without the prior written permission of both the copyright owner and the above publisher of this book. ✠ The scanning, uploading, and distribution of this book via the Internet or via any other means without the permission of the publisher is illegal and punishable by law. Please purchase only authorized electronic editions and do not participate in or encourage electronic piracy of copyrightable materials. Your support of the author's rights is appreciated. ✠ PHOTOGRAPHY Eric Hameister, Jesse James, and Frank Ockenfels TEXT Curtis Cummings ART DIRECTION/DESIGN Jaye Zimet PRODUCTION Grazyna Veras EDITORIAL Jennifer Ehmann MANAGING EDITORIAL Tory Klose ✠ 10 9 8 7 6 5 4 3 2 1

All photographs by Eric Hameister except the following: pp. 33–37 courtesy Jesse James; pp. 66, 67, 76–77, 92–93, 108–109 by Frank Ockenfels.

Jesse James, ass low and knees high, slams his ground-pounding custom chopper into third gear, cuts between two rumbling semis, and gasses the bike furiously through the gears into sixth. The chrome catches the coastal sun, lighting up the drab gray freeway. He flies wild toward the Long Beach skyline, but the ride is tame compared with the runaway train his life has been for the past three years.

Starting with a simple phone call from a cable TV channel—some kind of schoolroom educational channel no less—his life took a hard turn straight up into the stratosphere. Jesse was already one of the most notorious custom motorcycle builders in the country, having forged a distinctive style, an aggressive, nasty profile—both in bike and body. The call was from a producer, and he wanted to film Jesse creating a hand-built chopper for a special cable TV show called *Motorcycle Mania*.

"It won't be a big deal," the producer said. "We'll just follow you around with some cameras for a few weeks. Tape what you do around here."

Jesse thought for a minute. It might be good for business, but business was already good.

"What the hell. Sure. If you think John Q. Familyguy would be interested."

Jesse knew they would be interested.

A few short months later, *Motorcycle Mania* was by far the highest rated show the cable channel had aired in its entire nineteen-year history.

A sequel was ordered immediately, and Jesse was filmed building a new bike for the annual Sturgis Rally. *Motorcycle Mania 2* also shot to the top of the ratings and, like the first show, managed to capture something special in Jesse James. He was abrasive, foul mouthed, and wild. He was also talented, and he spoke straight, with no filter. Proud to be what he regarded as a simple metalworker, he demanded respect and took shit from no one. That strength came through loud and clear on television screens from coast to coast. This guy wasn't some pretty-boy media-created wannabe. Here, for once, the Real Deal struck a nerve.

Jesse James became more than a celebrity. He became an instant folk hero.

The big motor, stroked to 124 explosive cubic inches, blasts Jesse down the 710 freeway into San Pedro and away from the crowds, the television film crews, and the strangers wanting to shake his hand.

Thirty-three years old, with his own hit TV show, *Monster Garage*, and a reputation as a creative dynamo, the now-famous bike builder has been having trouble balancing his personal life with the constant tug of celebrity. He has had to hire a personal assistant to plan out his days minute by minute. He craves more time to work in his super-sized bike shop, West Coast Choppers, but the time has been getting harder to find. Having worked in the past as a bodyguard for various rock-and-roll bands, he has sampled firsthand the shoddy treatment that some of them had seen fit to dole out to their fans. When complete strangers started wanting to shake his hand and grab a quick snapshot, a flattered Jesse made it his policy to give away that minute or two whenever possible. Now, with much less free time at his disposal, he continues that practice.

The fans and well-wishers who crowd his motorcycle shop every day have never been anything but a positive influence for Jesse—the problem is everything else. He is reluctant to admit that outside factors and commitments are slowly squeezing the fun out of bike building. It's his identity and his greatest pride and joy. And there is one other thing on Jesse's mind.

Jesse James is in love.

Jesse's new girl is wild, tattooed, and crazy about her man. She's well known for her work in adult films, but that is now a closed chapter of her life. The love bug bit them both hard, and as far as his personal life goes, Jesse has never been happier. They've been together only a few months and are already talking about marriage.

She is every motorhead's dream—a sex-bomb beauty who's happy to sit in the corner of the garage while her man wrenches the hours away. She allows Jesse to work without interruption and is happy just to be there with him. As far as his new girl goes, he can't believe his luck.

Having achieved success beyond anything he could have hoped for, Jesse thinks this should be the best time of his life. But he's unsatisfied. Conquering the custom-bike world wasn't easy; it was a long, hard slog filled with sixteen-hour days and hostile reactions from the nonbelievers. West Coast Choppers has become *the* place to get a custom-built and the waiting list is a long one. But after years of turning out the baddest, most menacing choppers imaginable, Jesse feels like things are getting routine. He craves a challenge. Addicted to the creative act, he wants to push his skills to the limit, to increase his knowledge.

To sit still is to stagnate.

Copper.

For years there has been a vision of copper germinating in the back of Jesse's mind. As a child, in his father's antiques shop, the boy was drawn to the old copper household items strewn about the restoration shop. The metal has a primitive quality and can be polished to a blinding sheen. Jesse had planned to use copper in a custom bike a few years ago, but was sidetracked repeatedly by the bursting growth of his bike shop and his reputation.

Polished copper grabs sunlight like no other metal, and he's never seen a motorcycle fabricated with it.

Jesse gooses the throttle. He whips the bike back over the Vincent Thomas Bridge toward his shop. The stinging chill of the harbor city air clears the haze of frustration just enough to get through another week of constant demands from a hundred different directions.

But copper is again on his mind.

Fay Butler's workshop in Wheelright, Massachussets, looks as if it was plucked straight out of the nineteenth century. English wheels, mallets of all sizes, and power hammers are arranged throughout the shop. Skeletal wooden forms are stacked up in the corners. Fay Butler is one of the most expert metalsmiths in the world. Early in his career, Jesse sought his help in perfecting certain fabrication techniques. Now, world famous in his own right, Jesse is returning to one of his mentors for some further study.

Butler is a skilled coppersmith, one of the very few with a working knowledge of the special techniques necessary to form copper without ruining the metal. Copper is notoriously difficult to work because the metal's properties don't allow it to react predictably to normal steel-forming methods.

The coppersmith has agreed to take on Jesse once again as a pupil. Total opposites in personality, they share a common love for the work and exacting attention to detail.

At the dawn of Jesse's career, he had a brilliant idea. Instead of learning about the different types of fabrication from whomever he came across, why not look up the finest craftsmen and go to them? Fay Butler was at the top of Jesse's list from the beginning. His lessons here are difficult, but the long hours of false starts and mistakes are never a waste of time.

The learning process in any medium is littered with misguided attempts. To take the part of the attempt that was right and be able to separate it from what went wrong is progress in itself. Many is the bike builder who has learned more from what went wrong with a project than from what went right.

Jesse's new girl, who is now his fiancée, has come along on this trip. She can see how happy Jesse is to be working with his old friend again. She wants to be supportive and waits patiently while Fay takes Jesse through his coppersmith lessons. The two men realize that they are working in a nearly lost art, and Butler respects Jesse's thirst for acquiring this new skill.

After several days of intense study, Jesse begins to get a read on the metal's properties.

"I've always loved working the power hammer. To me it's a tool that has a soulful quality, and working it has always been a soulful process for me."

Under Butler's tutelage, Jesse eventually produces a small panel that he judges good enough for his projected Copper Bike.

"This is the first puzzle piece on the way to 100 miles an hour."

Butler judges Jesse's skills in coppersmithing advanced enough to take home to Long Beach. The student has made the teacher proud.

Who would have guessed that at the age of thirty-three, ex-juvenile delinquent Jesse James would almost become a teacher's pet?

Back in Long Beach, Jesse can't wait to try out his new copper-smithing chops. But first there're ten straight days of *Monster Garage* builds and business meetings and sponsorship deals and everything else.

A few weeks later, Jesse and his girl walk down the aisle in a beautiful glass church surrounded by pine trees overlooking the blue Pacific. Both smile openly at friends and family as they approach the altar. As Jesse slips the ring on his new wife's finger, some in the pews get ready to duck, just in case the glass church shatters as the groom moves in for the kiss.

Family members from both sides shake their heads, happy for the couple but aware that they both are hardheaded and used to getting their way.

Jesse and his new wife beam as they move up the aisle and out into their future together.

Up behind a large neon LIQUOR sign in the bowels of the West Coast Chopper shop is Jesse's private domain. No one is allowed up there. Illuminated by the red neon—ironic because Jesse is not a drinker—the fully equipped workshop is where Jesse escapes to pursue his personal projects. On this day he's working a sheet of copper into a fender for his new bike. He remembers Fay Butler's lessons. The notoriously difficult metal reluctantly submits to Jesse's will. His mind keeps wandering to the radical idea he has planned for the fuel tank. Rivet it together with no welding. He thinks that if executed with enough precision it could be leak free and stunning. He continues his work with a renewed focus until his mind wanders just long enough to let his other distraction enter.

He is troubled by the fact that he and his new wife have been having some pretty intense arguments. When things are good between them, it's absolutely the best. The electricity between them is palpable. But like in a John Lee Hooker song, when things are bad, they're really bad. When they fight, a black cloud hangs over them and usually over the whole shop. Everyone seems to be on edge, and he knows that it is bad for business.

He reminds himself that other people have had volatile relationships that have smoothed out over time and lasted, and he can't forget that when it's going well with her he's outright addicted. His thoughts are interrupted by a phone call. He normally does not take calls in his private workshop, but he recognizes the number. He reaches for the phone.

"Kid Motherf--king Rock."

Singer/songwriter Kid Rock and Jesse James are alike in a lot of ways. Both are media sensations in multiple fields. Both made it the hard way, emerging from humble beginnings to become pop culture sensations without the benefit of wealth or family connections. Both say exactly what they mean and live their lives without pretension. Both appreciate the things that money and fame can buy, but are grounded in their working-class background. Before they were buying big houses and Ferraris, they both knew what it was like to sweat utility bills every month.

Still, according to Bill Dodge, Jesse's longtime friend and right-hand man, "Jesse's always been a rock star—since he was a teenager. It was pretty clear to the kids who knew him." Everyone else is just now catching on.

Jesse calls Kid "my brother from another mother."

A Harley rider for years, Kid Rock has finally decided to have his friend build him a full balls-out custom. Though fully committed to the Copper Bike, Jesse agrees to take on the job with the simple statement "I'll make you something f--king cool."

Like Jesse, Kid (Bob or Bobby, to his friends) also has his hands full. He has just made a big jump from rap/metal superstar to conquering Nashville with a top-ten country ballad recorded with Sheryl Crow. He doesn't have time to discuss design ideas with Jesse, but he knows that his brother from the LBC will come up with something kickass special. He also knows Jesse well enough to see that the best work always gets done when the master builder is left to create what *he* wants, not what the client demands.

"I try to get to know the customer. What kind of music he listens to, what kind of car he drives. It's important to me that the bike fits the owner's personality. I never feel that a bike's profile is perfect until the rider is sittin' on it. It shouldn't look complete until the owner is a part of it."

Like anyone involved in serious creative process, Jesse works best when he's left alone.

"It's way better when the customer isn't poking his head in the shop every couple of weeks. When they do that I usually make the build take longer. I'll let 'em know when it's done."

Taking on the Kid Rock Bike while in the middle of the Copper Bike project stretches Jesse's already thin line of available shop time to the limit, and he still has to spend large blocks of his day on builds at the *Monster Garage* set, located in a nearby Long Beach warehouse.

Pit Boss/Shop Manager Bill Dodge and veteran builder Chopper Dave step up to make these bikes happen. Both are ace fabricators and good friends as well, used to pulling miracles out of thin air. And both are already overloaded with the long list of West Coast Choppers already on order with the shop. While most of the builders in the shop will contribute to the two high priority projects, Jesse knows that he can depend on Bill and Dave to tackle the tasks needing immediate attention.

Bill, known for his gruff demeanor, explains his focus like this, "You can be everyone's friend or you can get the f--king job done."

At home, things are still hot and cold with Jesse and his new wife. There are arguments. She is good at pushing buttons, and Jesse isn't known for letting things go by unopposed. Lately he has been distracted at the shop by the problems at home, a situation he finds completely unacceptable. He is used to fixing things. He's just gotta figure out how to adapt his talents to repairing his relationship with his wife.

While spending long hours hammering his frustrations out of copper, Jesse formulates a plan to get away. He's ridden virtually everywhere and wants to experience something completely new. He wants new pictures in his head from somewhere that will not trigger any memories of other phases of his life. And it's gotta be wide-open spaces. It's got to clear out the congestion that has been choking his life.

A cable channel has been trying to get Jesse to do a *Motorcycle Mania 3*. He's immune to cameras' being around, able to easily tune them out, and he wants to get the hell away from all of his daily distractions. He wants to go somewhere to recharge, where autograph seekers won't assault him everytime he gases up his bike. He remembers something about a colossal canyon in the middle of Mexico, much bigger than the Grand Canyon, that isn't very well known. It's called Barranca del Cobre—*Copper Canyon*.

Mexico. Copper Canyon. Inaccessible. Remote.

Jesse scans some sketches of Kid Rock's chopper project. It's going to be an absolutely badass menace to any road lucky enough to be run over with its fat Pirellis.

He picks up the phone. Kid Rock responds without hesitation. "Mexico? F--k ye-es, I'm in."

Jesse pauses in the shadows of his private custom projects' loft. Below him, blue-shirted fabricators buzz around a dozen bike lifts, wrenching, grinding, finessing parts into rolling art objects. Speed metal covers the normal sounds of men at work. Bill Dodge moves from lift to lift, checking progress, offering suggestions. Jesse's pit bull, Cisco, sniffs around. Tourists with cameras crowd into a gate for a look at the shop. He can hear the visitors talking. "Is Jesse here?" "Is that him over there?" "I wonder if Jesse's here?"

He turns away from the activity below and runs his hand across the virgin sheet of copper. He thinks about the overwhelming good fortune he has found through working with his hands. His fame had taken him to some strange places and has affected how people act around him. Jesse thinks about sitting in the greenroom at NBC studios, being silently amused by the young production assistants who scurried around asking him if there was anything they could get for him. No, he didn't have any special dietary or vegetarian requirements. The sandwich tray was fine. He heard his name called out, the audience cheered, and Jesse James laughed to himself at the surreal nature of fame.

Be it Leno, Conan, Kimmel, or Letterman, Jesse's message is basi-

...any the same—yes, all this attention is great. Yeah, I was voted one of *People* magazine's sexiest men by a bunch of people who've never met me. And yeah, sometimes I use bad language. But seriously Dave/Jay/Conan/Jimmy, I'm just a welder, a blue-collar, Dickies-wearin' metalfabber.

Jesse studies a large wall calendar marked with what is planned for every day of the coming month, broken down into hours. Personal appearances and *Monster Garage* commitments have taken a serious bite out of his shop time. All he can think is that there are too many boxes with *Jesse New York, Jesse Detroit, Jesse Meeting with Sponsors, Jesse—Two Interviews.*

His mind moves to Mexico. Open country. Endless highways.

He retreats to his loft and again concentrates on the problems he will have to overcome in constructing a fuel-tight copper tank using only rivets instead of welds. He thinks he can make it work, but the precision involved is like nothing he has ever tried before. He goes to work and actually makes some good progress, when he is interrupted.

"Jesse, the missus is on line two."

He sighs, remembering the tremendous argument they had had before he left the house that morning.

"I'll call her back."

Jesse concentrates on the difficult fabrication, forming and cutting the tank sections. Many hours later the fuel tank is almost ready for the rivets.

Once again a phone call.

Jesse, Kid Rock is on the line.

The tired builder picks up the line.

"Bobby."

Kid's voice is excited.

"Hey bro, how'd ya like to come chill out with me in Iraq for a couple days?"

For the first time that day, Jesse cracks a smile.

The morning sun casts a golden glow over Baghdad. Flying high enough to avoid small-arms fire, the air force C-130 transport plane crosses over the Tigris and Euphrates rivers en route to a military base still unnamed for security reasons. The pilots, fans of West Coast Choppers, allow Jesse to watch from the cockpit. They tell Jesse they're not happy that the plane is full of VIPs because they have to fly easy. They want to show him what the plane can do balls out. Jesse learns that "balls out" or "balls to the wall" is an old air force term from when bombers had four throttle levers capped with plastic balls. Shoving them fully forward toward the bulkhead wall gave maximum throttle, hence the term.

The city looks dusty and hot and the welder from Long Beach can make out palm trees and a few wrecked buildings. Mostly, though, it looks like a big city in the middle of the desert just waking up to a new day.

Kid Rock has managed to smuggle Jesse in as his tour manager for some USO appearances. A few weeks before, Jesse had been sent a photograph of an armored vehicle from a couple of enlisted WCC fans deployed to the desert war zone. They had painted a giant West Coast Choppers Maltese cross logo across the front of their vehicle. Jesse is hoping to be able to find them while he is in Iraq. He wants to thank...

them for their support and maybe hang out with them for a little while. He has brought a copy of the photograph to help him.

Jesse takes a seat as the big cargo plane descends steeply to land at the desert air base. He listens as the plane touches down and the four 1800-horsepower engines rev hard before throttling back for the taxi in. Studying the cavernous interior of the plane, Jesse admires the skeletal internal structure of the fuselage. Metal fabricators just like him built this plane, maybe even at one of the aircraft plants back in Long Beach.

Across from him, Kid Rock sleeps in one of the uncomfortable seats. His signature felt hat is pulled down low and his black stars and bars T-shirt reads TWO GREAT DANIELS—CHARLEY AND JACK. Even in the dark plane, the Iraqi sun heats up the cabin quick.

Jesse calls to his sleeping friend.

"Hey, Bob."

"Huh?"

"Bob, wake up."

"What?"

"Balls out has nothing to do with testicles."

"Huh?"

Jesse knew that Kid Rock would be mobbed wherever he went, but he is actually a bit surprised by the attention that he himself has been generating. The soldiers have been stationed in a strange land for months, basically quarantined on their bases, and they're hungry to talk to anyone who has news from or any connection to back home.

"They're so glad just to look at someone in civilian clothes."

The soldiers keep repeating to Jesse how much they appreciate the show of support from back home. On many levels, this deployment is exceptionally isolating for the people in uniform.

"We had some limited interaction with the Iraqis, drivers and stuff like that. We got a few of them to put up the horned hand. They were okay—had no idea who we were, but they seemed happy to see us. Soldiers kept callin' out my name when they saw me. I felt weird that they all wanted my autograph and wanted pictures with me. I felt like it was me that wanted my picture taken with all of them. My life is blessed; they're the ones making sacrifices every day."

Unfortunately, all inquiries about the West Coast Chopper tank come up empty. No one is able to locate the tank or the crewmen who had sent the picture.

Jesse decides to keep the photo tacked to the wall at the shop. Hopefully, the soldiers will show up there once they make rotation back Stateside.

On the plane bound for home, leaving deprived troops and a deprived country behind him, Jesse counts his blessings and makes a vow to himself to make his marriage work.

At the shop, work on the Copper Bike has finally kicked into high gear. The fenders are finished and Jesse is hard at work on the supertrick exhaust shrouds. The copper oil tank is next. The components are works of sculpture on their own. Jesse pictures how everything will look bolted together as he moves across the shop to check on the progress of another knock-'em-out feature of the Copper Bike.

Jesse is having the one-of-a-kind wheels cut out of solid blocks of billet aluminum. Each wheel will take an astounding, budget-melting fifty-eight hours of precision cutting in his new CNC machine.

"These wheels would cost twenty-five grand to send out and have done. I like owning my own machines because I can do really f--ked-up stuff like this, then put them on a motorcycle and abuse 'em."

Jesse inspects some custom brackets that Chopper Dave has been fabricating for Kid Rock's bike. Impressed by what he sees, Jesse hands them back.

Instead of complimenting the fine work, Jesse walks away grinning and quietly saying, "I hate Chopper Dave because he had a mullet in high school."

Outside the shop, his new wife's black Hummer comes to a stop. Bill and Chopper Dave roll their eyes. From his upstairs loft, Jesse watches his beautiful wife climb out of the massive vehicle. So far they've had a good week.

He hopes that the two of them are going to make it through another afternoon without any button pushing or voice raising.

Down in the shop, Bill and Chopper Dave stick to their tasks and hope for the same thing.

They're not optimistic.

Jesse and his wife decide to see a marriage counselor. Things between them improve for a week, then it's back to mood swings, nasty phone calls, and general chaos.

One WCC employee says: "I think she truly wants to be there to support and inspire Jesse. But she just can't help herself, she gets going, then he gets going, and all the emotional stuff does just the opposite of what it should do. It tears them both up."

Then there is a string of good days where the love seems as strong as ever and with it optimism that everything will work out between them. The chaser to that sweet drink of nectar, of course, is a week of anger and shouting.

Jesse can't figure out what's going wrong.

"I dunno. It's pillow talk to nuclear war in, like, half a second."

The perpetual Long Beach sun burns down on the West Coast Choppers parking lot. The black primer bakes on the decal-encrusted customs and pickup trucks of the WCC employees. The regular crowd of tourists and visitors is spread out across the lot and in the main showroom, taking snapshots of recently completed choppers, hot rods, and *Monster Garage* projects.

A sweet, lowered Benz, windows tinted dark, rolls to a stop outside the shop gate. The visitors and tourists watch closely to see if it might be one of those Hollywood celebrities that they hear tend to hang out around here. The glossy black Benz's door swings open and a shirtless Kid Rock steps out of the car. He says hello to the small crowd while pulling on a shirt with F--K YOU silk-screened in large letters across the back. He finishes off the white-trash-rock-star-hillbilly outfit with a dirty bent-up John Deere trucker hat.

He patiently signs a few autographs and smiles for a few photos. As he makes his way to the metal workshop gate, he hears a middle-age tourist in short pants and brown socks ask his wife, "Is he an actor? What show's he on?"

Kid pauses and with a grin declares what is sort of his usual greeting, "I'm Kid Motherf--kin' Rock, Motherf--ker!"

Jesse and Cisco meet him at the gate and together they disappear into the dark.

Bill pushes Kid's bike into the center of the shop's work area.
"Here you go, Bob. Get this thing outta here."
The bike is a shock, even to Kid Rock.
All he can say is, "Oh, jeez."

It's a total stunner. He walks around the chopper speechless, stopping to study the details. Chrome frame with fuel tank and fenders in *Dukes of Hazzard* orange. Deep flames all over. Black wheels. A small General Lee Dodge Charger painted on the rear fender.

Bill and Jesse know that Kid owns one of the original *Dukes* TV show cars.

The seat is hand-cut and tooled leather with the name of his latest record spelled out.

It says: AMERICAN BAD ASS.

Jesse looks at his speechless head-shaking friend.

"We're gonna take this one to Mexico."

"F--k yes we are, homes!" grins Kid.

Jesse is given a copy of a custom parts catalog put out by a well-known builder. The pages are littered with almost exact copies of WCC parts—fuel tanks, fenders, exhausts. Some are altered just enough to make them lame, a degree or two less threatening than the WCC originals. This kind of copycatting and wussification of his designs has been going on for years.

"I suppose I should be flattered," the tired builder quips as the catalog drops into an elaborately pinstriped garbage can. "But I'm not."

Jesse sits back in his private loft and admires the just finished fuel tank, ready to be mounted on the Copper Bike. The riveting process had taken hours of painstaking precision work. It looks like it belongs in a museum as an example of fine art from another age. It went together just as Jesse had predicted it would. Not a single weld.

The exhausted craftsman picks up a cup of liquid and pauses before pouring it into the tank. He runs his hands one more time over the tight, perfectly spaced rivets. He pours in the liquid, then sloshes it around. He inspects the copper beauty for what seems like forever.

No leaks whatsoever.

Down on the shop floor the nearly completed Copper Bike chassis stands reflecting the neon light wildly across the walls of the busy assembly area. The bike is built around the new WCC Dominator frame, the first one of its kind. It is waiting for a finishing touch that Jesse is cradling as he climbs down the metal staircase.

It is almost ready for its rider.

The Copper Bike is finished literally hours before Bill has to load it into a van alongside Kid's orange hillbilly hot rod. Jesse has brought in Hot Dog, a favorite painter of his, to lay down some lettering in a Carrera Panamerica/LBC to Mexico theme. He finishes the top of the tank with the crossed flags of the WCC Maltese cross and Mexican tricolor.

There has been no time for any kind of shakedown, only a half-mile spurt through Long Beach to try to make sure everything's going to work properly south of the border.

Jesse flies to El Paso to hook up with Kid and the documentary camera crew. They agree on a route that will take them from mean, murderous narco-plagued Juárez through the heart of Mexico, avoiding big cities and concentrating on the vast undeveloped interior of the country. On the map, the twisted lines make it clear that riding to Copper Canyon is going to take some concentration.

"Bad roads. Rigid frame. Big fun."

Back in Long Beach, Bill Dodge fueled up and loaded with a quarter million dollars' worth of custom choppers strapped down behind him, warms up the WCC van's hot-rodded V-8. Photographer Eric Hameister climbs in on the shotgun side and is told to buckle up. They've got to meet Jesse and a film crew in Texas and they don't have time to lollygag. Bill lights a fat Cuban and starts his banzai run to El Paso.

Things were tense with his wife as Jesse packed for the Mexico trip. When the argument started, he paused, bit his lip, and saw this as one of the main reasons he had to get away and clear his head. After telling her that he would see her when he got back, he made for the door. As he stepped through he heard her say that she loved him and that she would miss him.

He didn't turn his head.

Now he sat in his hotel room with his cell phone in his hand. Putting it away, he shifts his focus to Mexico.

Bill and Hameister roll the WCC transport van into the Texas rallying point with time to spare. The film crew watch the men climb out of the bug-encrusted van. They had just made the Long Beach to El Paso run in ten hours flat. Hameister stretches his back.

"Jesus Christ. We got out of LA and that needle didn't dip below 100 miles per hour the whole way here. Nonstop. Andretti there's a fiend."

Bill rubs his neck and lights a fresh cigar.

For years the Carrera Panamerica was one of the premier auto races in the world. Almost fifty years ago, to celebrate the opening of the Panamerican Highway, the Mexican president invited all the top car manufacturers to compete in a grueling race that spanned the entire length of Mexico. Gargantuan V-8 Cadillacs and Hudson Hornets roared down the new highway leaving squashed tarantulas and traumatized Gila monsters in their earthshaking wake. The big American cars outlasted the smaller, lighter European sports models and dominated the event for years.

Now Jesse James and Kid Rock are about to launch their own attack on the Mexican roadways. But it doesn't start well straight out of the gate. They've been waiting in a cross-border cantina for the bikes to show up. Bill Dodge, who rocketed a transport van halfway across the United States in ten hours flat, has been held up at the border with a paperwork nightmare. Kid sips a beer in a Juárez cantina while Jesse watches the busy street outside. So far, they haven't been recognized.

"Bill's gotta be going out of his mind. He hates bureaucracy."

It takes seven hours for Mexican officials to clear up all the necessary documents and release the bikes. It's clear that the group is staying in Juárez for the night. After catching a meal, Jesse turns in early. Kid Rock and some of the crew head into town for *cervezas* and some rounds of pool.

It's 8:00 A.M. and the heavy Mexican air is already heating up. The WCC Expeditionary Force is assembling at the designated rendezvous point. One of the film crew guys rubs his temples and says something about seeing daylight breaking outside a nightclub. All he can remember from the night before is Kid Rock's voice calling out, "*Una cerveza más, por favor.*"

As if on cue, Kid arrives, looking fresh and ready to roll. He had just seen a couple minutes of *Sling Blade* on the hotel big screen. He unleashes a pitch-perfect Billy Bob impression.

"'Ah sure do laake them french fried potaters. Um-huh.'"

Jesse ambles up right behind him, unleashing his own Billy Bob interpretation.

"'Some peoples call it a Kaiser blade. Ah call it a sling blade. Uh-huh.'"

Bill meets the group and emerges from the transport van cool as a cucumber. This trip is just one more project to oversee for him.

"Let's get this f--kin' sightseeing tour rollin'."

Out come the bikes. Kid climbs onto his first, fires the engine, and pulls on his gloves. Wearing a white wife beater and baggy trousers, the rap-metal-country-billy-rock star warms up his new chopper in a glare of chrome and flamed *Dukes*-boy orange. Jesse wraps a bandanna around his head. A crowd is beginning to form. American tourists are pulling out cameras. The Copper Bike looks proud and agile despite its exaggerated proportions. The engine fires perfectly and immediately settles into a steady idle. From the crossed flags to the devil seat rivets to the polished copper shining brilliantly in the early morning sun, the Copper Chopper was made for Mexico. Jesse drops it into first gear and it's *hasta la vista* to *los estados unidos.*

The WCC Expeditionary Task Force makes its first move toward the heart of Mexico.

The Mexican desert is hot—hotter than a scorpion's ass—but Jesse and Kid eat up the rough highway without breaking a sweat. A hundred miles in and the bikes are rumbling hard through country rolling with sagebrush and sand dunes. Once out of the populated areas, there are few vehicles and no unending line of billboards to obscure the vistas. This is exactly what Jesse needs. No accounting for every minute of his time. No constant backup of phone calls and e-mails to return. No ridiculous Southern California traffic. And no helmet laws.

The two riders are free to go as far and as fast as they want. The schedule is loose, so they can stop to check out anything that looks interesting. The enormous pressure of running a multimillion-dollar business, being a bona fide media star, and finishing two intricate and difficult bike builds is already beginning to evaporate. His personal life will hopefully be dealt with somewhere on the expanse of the ragged Mexican roadway. Even the 90-degree heat feels good.

During one of the desert rest stops, the guys on the crew spring a surprise on the two bikers. They manage to arrange for some quad racers to arrive at some particularly inviting nearby sand dunes. Jesse and Kid take some time out to tear through the desert and launch themselves airborne over the wind-swept dunes, either totally confident or so intent on blowing off steam that neither of them thinks about a broken bone or sprained ankle putting an end to the road trip before it gets started.

As Kid and Jesse get the competitive juices flowing and try to one-up each other on the speeding quads, the crew starts to worry about an imminent injury to one or both of the bikers, but soon they have a bigger problem on their hands.

Two carloads of *federales* have crept up on the party and everyone becomes worried about what is about to happen. They are toting assault weapons and approach Jesse and Kid. The crew starts wondering how bad the food will be in a Mexican jail, sure that Jesse is going to say something to land them all behind bars.

The policemen and the bikers talk for a few minutes. For all anyone knows this could be some kind of national park off limits to any kind of off-road vehicle.

Then something happens that could only occur in *la vida loca* of Jesse James. The *federales* hand over their assault weapons to the two bikers, who then jack rounds into the chambers and start shooting at a pile of old auto parts in the distance. Soon they are setting up Coke cans and water bottles. The *pistolas* come out and the cops and kids laugh through some target practice.

Jesse shrugs his shoulders. His Spanish is pretty spotty.

"Hey, they heard we were riding through and they're fans. I don't think they have to account for their bullets."

After blowing through a few hundred rounds, blasting anything they could find for a target, Jesse and Kid shake hands with the lawmen, pose with them for a few pictures, and part ways. The *federales* climb into their patrol cars and set off for destinations unknown. As they pass the group of incredulous gringos, their hands come out with the universal two-fingered sign of *la mano hornuda*.

Jesse grins at the crew as he fires up his hand-built copper masterpiece. The next town is a good clip ahead. They're gonna have to move if they're gonna make it by sundown.

It's **92 degrees** at 8:00 A.M. Once again, Kid Rock was the last one to bed—last reported location a cantina at 3:00 A.M. But now he's up and ready to go at the designated start time. Someone mumbles about losing money at a cock fight. The crew marvels at Kid's fortitude while questioning how many nights he will be able to keep it up. He launches into his Billy Bob voice.

"Ah lahke motels with no running water. Uh-huh."

The day's ride would blast through Chihuahua and wind up in the mountains, within striking distance of Copper Canyon.

Again out on the highway, the riders rapidly blow past car after car, not one of them with a straight edge on it, until the highway becomes empty. Even with a camera truck nearby, the highway seems desolate. Adding to the remoteness of the group, their one and only satellite phone works only sporadically. Occasionally Jesse and Kid have to brake hard to avoid smacking into a wandering horse or one of the many free-ranging cows that tend to wander across the highway. This kind of simplicity is one of the things the two famous gringos came to Mexico to find.

Every few hours, the group, needing fuel and cold drinks, stops in a small sun-bleached Chihuahua town. Most of them blend together, but all share a more primitive personality. No running water. Butchers leave meat outside with no refrigeration. Squawking chickens in the street. Time stands still in Mexico.

Jesse and Kid cause a commotion in every town. No one knows

their identities, most assume that they are soccer stars. The bikes are mobbed by peasants that have never seen anything like them. Young men inspect them wide eyed. Shy girls in elaborate costume stand a respectful distance away, but are curious just the same.

Local cops are summoned to investigate the disturbance that the two crazy gringo soccer players are causing. They move in for a closer look at the bikes, smile, "*Bueno,*" and move on.

Standing proud next to the locals, Jesse's Copper Bike looks like something out of Sam Peckinpah's *The Wild Bunch*. It's clear that the chopper is in its element both out on the rough roads and in the small isolated towns.

Jesse and Kid love the anonymity of the situation. When asked in broken English who he is, Kid responds with something like "Hank Williams" or "Berry Gordy."

Stocked up on fuel and snacks, the twosome head out on the road, leaving the sleepy town to wonder what the hell those gringos with the beautiful motorbikes are all about.

Never one for conventional macho motorcycle gear, since day one of the trip Jesse has been wearing what look like cheap jail-issue slippers. Kid is wearing some as well, though he's stenciled OZZY in ballpoint pen onto his pair. The camera crew has been watching the open belt drive on the Copper Bike spin for days like some kind of dangerous industrial tool just inches from Jesse's unprotected foot. Jesse is unconcerned.

"For this bike, the belt drive just had to be fully exposed. It just fit the spirit of the whole thing. You just have to think about what you're doin' and don't let your foot slip."

Jesse nods at his hard-core biker slippers: "Three dollars. Wal-Mart."

No one mentions the condition of the Mexican roads or the bumps and unpatched holes that sometimes send both riders bouncing in their hand-stitched leather seats.

One of the appeals of a long motorcycle ride is the juxtaposition of the solitary nature of the ride to the physicality of being fully exposed to the elements and anyone else sharing the road. Even in a group of ten riders, each biker is left to his own thoughts without small talk or radio stations to distract him.

Danger, of course, is always hovering nearby, an integral part of the soul of motorcycling. This soul is quantumly enhanced by the physics of a lightweight overpowered chopper with minimal suspension. The mind can't fly off into the clouds; the eyes and focus must be kept on the road. Still, there is plenty of time to think.

The long ride is a metaphor for both Jesse's and Kid Rock's lives. Fame puts anyone under a microscope, yet both are private people with depth that can be obscured by the surface flash.

The time spent crossing the Mexican heartland on essentially empty highways, powering through visions of great poverty and stunning natural beauty, transmits a spiritual message that cannot be denied, even to the most heathen among the group. The energy conveyed from the massive undeveloped spaces and the passing indigenous people affects each traveler differently. But the farther into the interior Jesse and Kid ride, the more quiet they become at the rest stops.

Just before they begin their ascent into the mountains, rain clouds form overhead, darkening the sky. A bright concentrated shaft of sunlight paints the road ahead of the two riders. The beauty of the sky and country at that moment etches itself into everyone's memory. Later Jesse would talk about that stretch of highway.

"I felt like I could've gone down that particular road forever. The way the sun was shining through the clouds—I felt like I was connected. Like veins were coming through the handlebars into my hands and my blood was circulating through the bike as I went through it. The faster I went, the faster my heart pumped, and the slower I went the more relaxed I was. And it was a direct reflection—the motor RPMs were in tune with my heart rate and it was part of me. It was good."

The day's final leg up to the small town of Creel, high in the Sierra Madres, sees both Kid and Jesse riding with a peacefulness suggesting that all the chaos and unrealistic demands put on their lives have melted away. Every jolt of the rough Mexican roads has jarred a little bit of poison out of their systems.

A few miles shy of the town, the two riders pull into an old mountain cemetery. The air has chilled with the elevation and both are wearing leather jackets, almost looking like conventional bikers for the first time. The sun has gone down and they just want some quiet time for a few minutes before roaring into the nearby town.

They sit on a marble slab next to some graves draped with fresh flowers. Jesse tells stories about some of the crazy shenanigans that have been acted out at the WCC shop when deadlines and pressure get the whole crew operating out on the ragged edge. Kid talks about life on the road, a life that also drives everyone to extreme behavior after twenty or thirty cities are behind them. Attracted to the camera lights, large bats start swooping down on their reflective moment.

They take that as a good sign, fire up the bikes, make a quick tour of the cemetery, and move out toward their waiting hotel rooms.

Creel is known for its population of Tarahumara, an indigenous tribe that has lived in the mountains for thousands of years. It is right on the edge of the mountain ranges that converge to make Copper Canyon.

For some reason Creel has also become a pilgrimage destination for European hippies. The cobblestone streets are full of dark-skinned locals dressed in traditional clothing walking alongside pale transients with matted hair and Birkenstock sandals.

The Eurohippies' buzz is seriously hushed by the two oversized and undermuffled choppers rolling into town. Jesse looks at Kid.

"What, they bury Jerry Garcia up here?"

Once again, Kid Rock is the last one to bed. His familiar request, "Una cerveza más, por favor," had been heard all over the little town. And again in the morning, he's right on time, a little bit squint eyed, shuffling up the street with a few local kids running around behind him. One of the crew blurts out what everyone is thinking.

"How the hell can he party until four A.M. every night and then be here ready to ride at eight?"

Jesse slips on his wraparound shades and fires up his big chopper.

"He's a rock star. That's what they do. It's how they live. He doesn't have to wake up in the morning. My mind-set is still in wake-up-and-start-welding mode."

Copper Canyon is one of six massive canyons formed by two hundred gorges. Four times the size of the Grand Canyon in Arizona, it is an unsung wonder of the world. Its breathless beauty is unknown to most people north of the border, and that's probably a good thing. There are none of the crowding problems that plague the Grand Canyon, and no land developers are trying to build ridiculous structures next to it. It stands in proud grandeur, swallowing up everything topographical for hundreds of miles around it. The indigenous peoples have always considered it the cradle of the gods.

Kid and Jesse stand at the edge of a thousand-foot-tall wall of stone. They look out over the vast system of gorges. The air is cool in their lungs. Both are silent, burning the view into their minds. They both know that they will never see anything like it again.

Jesse concentrates on the wondrous panorama in front of him and finds that he can only think about his wife waiting for him at home. He wishes she were there to see it with him.

The two men walk along the rim of the canyon. The sun, low on the horizon, throws an orange glow onto the copper-colored lichen that grow on the canyon walls.

As they walk in silence, Jesse searches for the point of the long road trip. There had been no spiritual awakening; those only come to the ones who are searching for it.

They had made it here. That was the point. The journey is always more important than the destination. It had been a great f--king ride. And it wasn't over yet.

La espina del diablo—the Spine of the Devil—is a primitive twisting road leading down from the Sierra Madres to the town of Hermosillo at the foot of the mountains. The three hundred miles of sheer-drop cliffs, fallen boulders, blind switchbacks, and white knuckling danger is, in a way, a good preparation for the return to the Los Angeles basin. The fourteen hours it takes to transverse it is about as mind numbing as a couple of hours in LA traffic.

The dusty road eats up a solid day. Anytime the road opens up enough to make a decent pace, a switchback appears out of nowhere, usually with a large boulder blocking half the road.

"I keep waiting for Wile E. Coyote to drop an anvil in front of me," Jesse quips.

The bikes are being trucked down in the WCC van. To try to ride down the Spine of the Devil wouldn't have been fun or relaxing or spiritual or anything but miserable.

Eric Hameister sums it up this way: "At first it's kind of like a video game with obstacles popping out everywhere to avoid, but that excitement ends quick and then you just realize that you're looking at three hundred miles of second gear."

Finally, the distant lights of Hermosillo appear, meaning only one thing to the WCC Expeditionary Task Force—a hot meal and a bed.

Tumbling out of the vehicles outside their hotel, the whole crew feels like they've just gone ten rounds. Even Kid Rock turns in early.

The final day of the Mexico trip is a fast ride to the Sea of Cortez. To honor the end of the ride, the camera crew meets Kid and Jesse wearing Mexican wrestling masks. As the two choppers accelerate onto the highway, Blue Demon, Anibal, Mil Mascaras, and El Santo try to keep up.

Traffic on the highway increases the closer they get to the coast. People honk horns and wave to the two bikers. At a fuel stop, Jesse thinks he can smell the sea air up ahead.

"I could never live too far away from the ocean. Even if I don't see it for days at a time back home, I can always feel it there."

The hard-charging copper speed machine and the orange *Dukes-boy* hot rod arrive in San Carlos in time to catch the sun setting over the water in a brilliant show of orange and red. Looking out over the water at a few small fishing boats and miles of open shoreline, it's clear that they're not back home yet.

Jesse thinks of the past few days. Riding through towns without a single car in sight. Old farmers with cracked faces and ruined hands. Black-eyed girls in traditional dresses watching silently from across dusty streets. Long stretches of untamed desert vistas. Magnificent mountain ranges.

A woman who said she'd miss him waiting for him at home.

In town that night, Kid Rock and some of the crew hit the restaurants and cantinas with a vengeance. Later the group ends up in Kid's hotel room. Strumming his guitar, he kicks it with his small audience, drinking beer and singing Johnny Cash and Merle Haggard songs until the early hours of the morning.

Six hours later, Jesse parks his '54 next to the black Hummer and walks to the back door of his beach house. Before he can slide his key into the lock, the door swings open. His new bride, eyes bright with love and longing, pulls him inside.

In his office above the motorcycle and hot rod-packed showroom at West Coast Choppers, Jesse and his wife talk quietly and study a lightbox strewn with transparencies to be used in an upcoming WCC calendar. They choose the best images, slide them into protective sleeves, and together plan the next shoot. Both seem relaxed. *Monster Garage* resumes shooting the next day, and they both want to go home to a quiet evening alone.

Jesse returned from Mexico two weeks ago, batteries fully charged and ready to look at his life in the reflection of all the good things in it.

"Mexico makes you appreciate simple things like running water and bathrooms."

The couple promises that they won't let the petty day-to-day headaches pile up until the pressure forces an explosion.

The footage from the road trip is good, Kid is back on tour, and Jesse is ready for the pace to accelerate again. His personal assistant breaks down his days into reserved blocks of time.

Everything is holding together.

But a month later it is finished. Flying vases. Cops. Restraining orders.

Jesse and his wife both wanted their marriage to work. In a real relationship the natural human inclination is to concentrate on the good times and let the bad times go. But when chaos becomes the rule, the days can only become numbered. Passion plays at three in the morning get old very quickly. Especially when the alarm clock goes off at six.

"It's bad enough dealing with hoodlums in the LBC who want to kick my ass, and then having to pick up a telephone in the office to fight off some kind of predatory business threat. I have zero desire to come home to find a f--kin' war in the kitchen. Or the bedroom."

The good times slip too far away, until they're out of reach, and the only thing left to grasp is disappointment and anger.

Jesse, known for swift, decisive judgment calls, pulls the brake lever on the carousel of chaos.

"She got her pink slip. Taped to her locker." Decision final.

He strokes Cisco's head and does a little self-evaluation.

"Note to self—never marry a porn star."

Jesse looks to the Copper Bike, parked a few feet away in the shop next to a large power hammer. It is a landmark bike for Jesse, and not just because of the trip through Mexico. With that bike, Jesse responded to a challenge of his own, to force himself to master new skills and to then execute those skills in an artful and expert manner.

What started in a Massachusetts workshop, the small piece of hand-formed copper—the first puzzle piece on the way to 100 miles per hour—now stands triumphantly bathed in neon, a few feet away from its proud creator. In finished form it has emerged as one of the finest motorcycle customs ever created in terms of beauty, intricacy, cohesive design, and level of difficulty.

Push the bar up and while trying for it, elevate yourself.

In a world of false heroes and media stars with smiles as phony as their cosmetic surgery, Jesse James has emerged from the sparks of a welding torch to take an important position in the national consciousness. He's not just a talented welder with an attitude that every wage slave wishes he could adopt. He's kicking the lameness out of everything he comes in contact with. False hipsters are out. The Real Thing is in.

The Jesse James plan for world domination hurtles forward. Acquiring knowledge and continually mastering new skills will make it happen.

Jesse pulls his beloved '54 Chevy into the parking lot at WCC headquarters. It's early and tourists are already milling about. A couple of home-built choppers are parked nearby, their riders gazing at him through dark wraparound sunglasses. Cisco the pitbull wags his nub of a tail from behind the steel mesh gate closing off the shop area.

Jesse pauses before opening the door of the black-primed custom, scanning the crowd of visitors, knowing that he won't be able to take three steps before someone will want an autograph or a photo.

"This is, like, Graceland for bikers."

He exits the lowered custom and takes two steps before the crowd moves toward him.

Fay Butler is one of the most expert metal-smiths in the world.

"my life is blessed : they're the ones making sacrifices, " every day.

مدينة الكويت

Kuwait City

طريق
40

copper. has a primitive quality and can be polished to a blinding sheen.

the
notoriously
difficult
metal
reluctantly
submits to
Jesse's will.

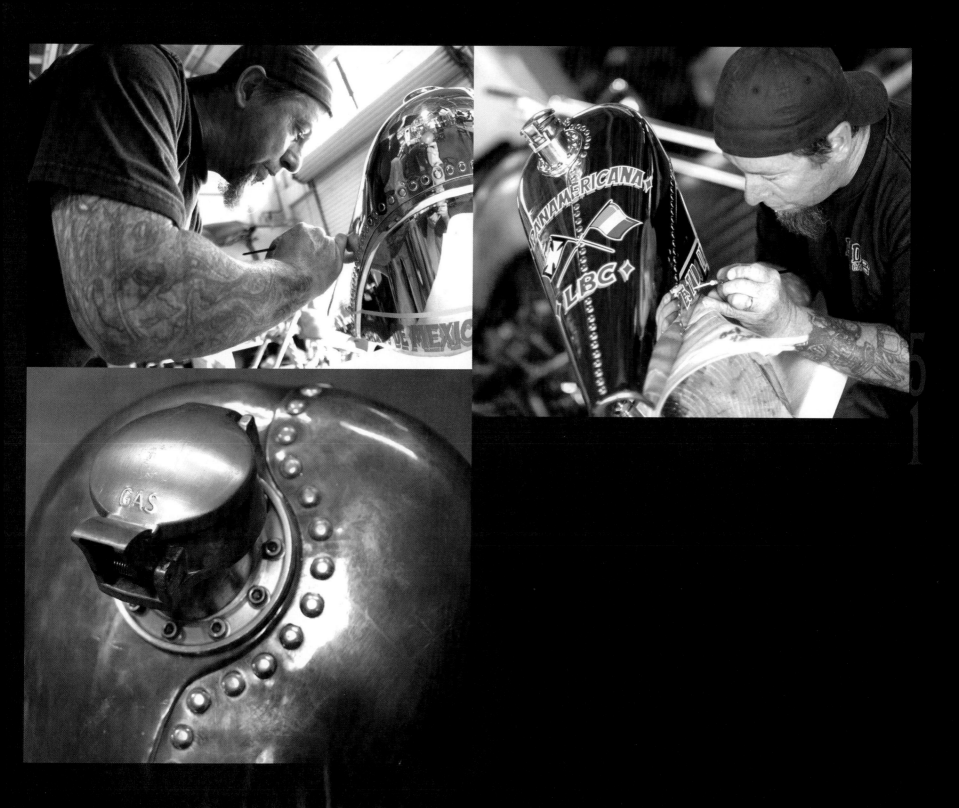

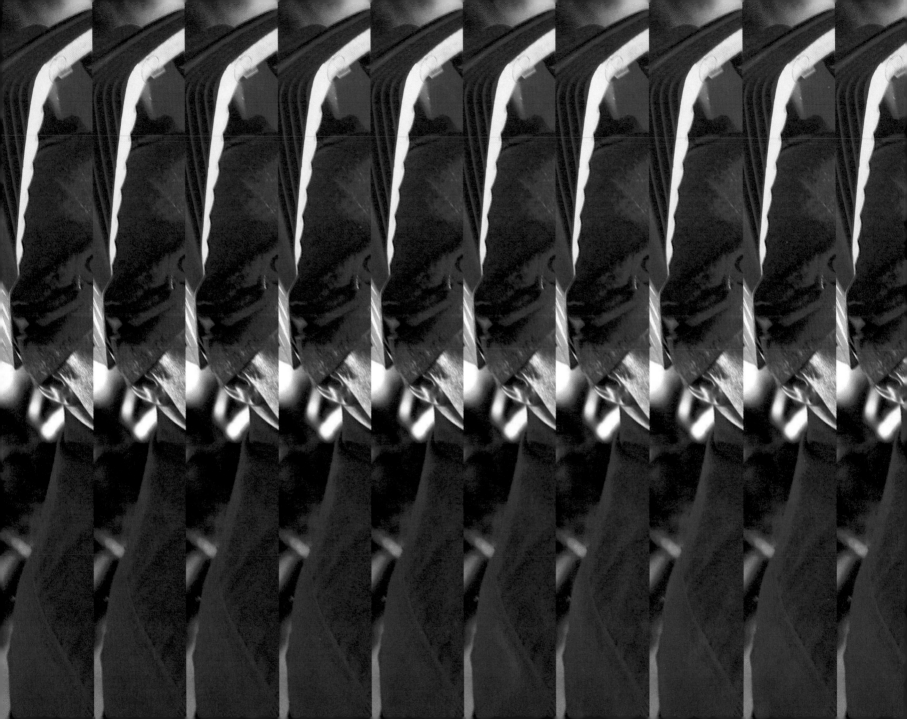

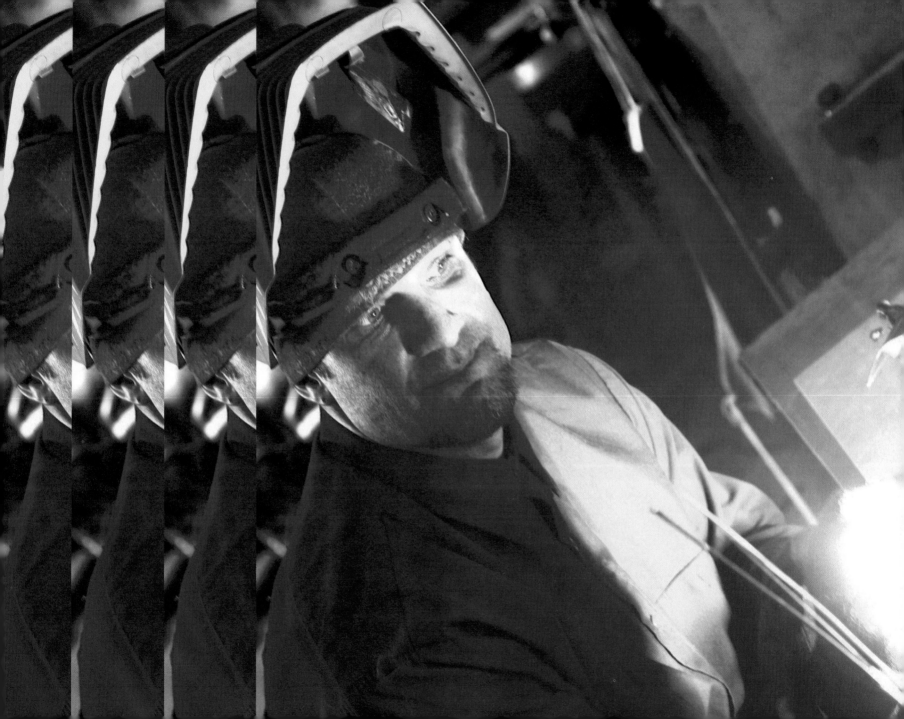

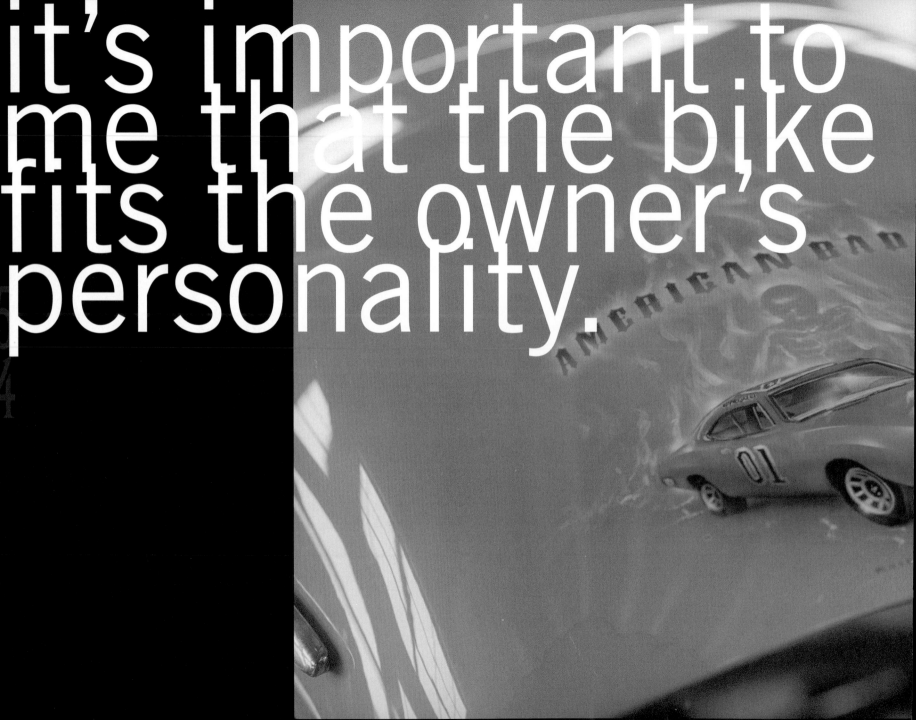

it's important to me that the bike fits the owner's personality.

all he
can say is,,
"oh, jeez."

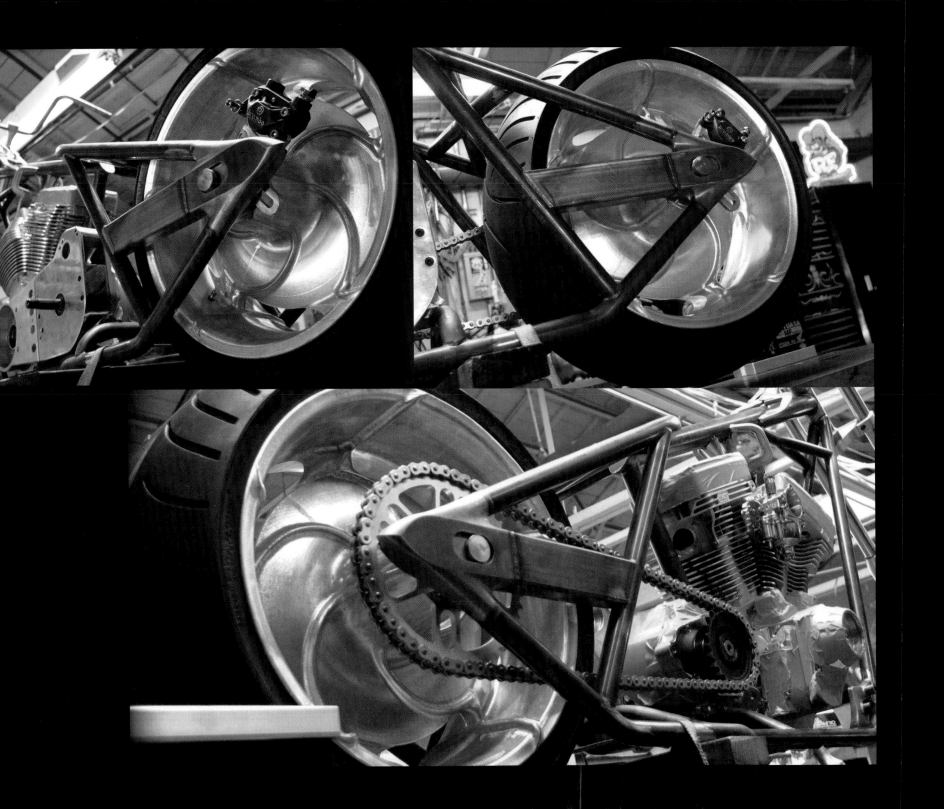

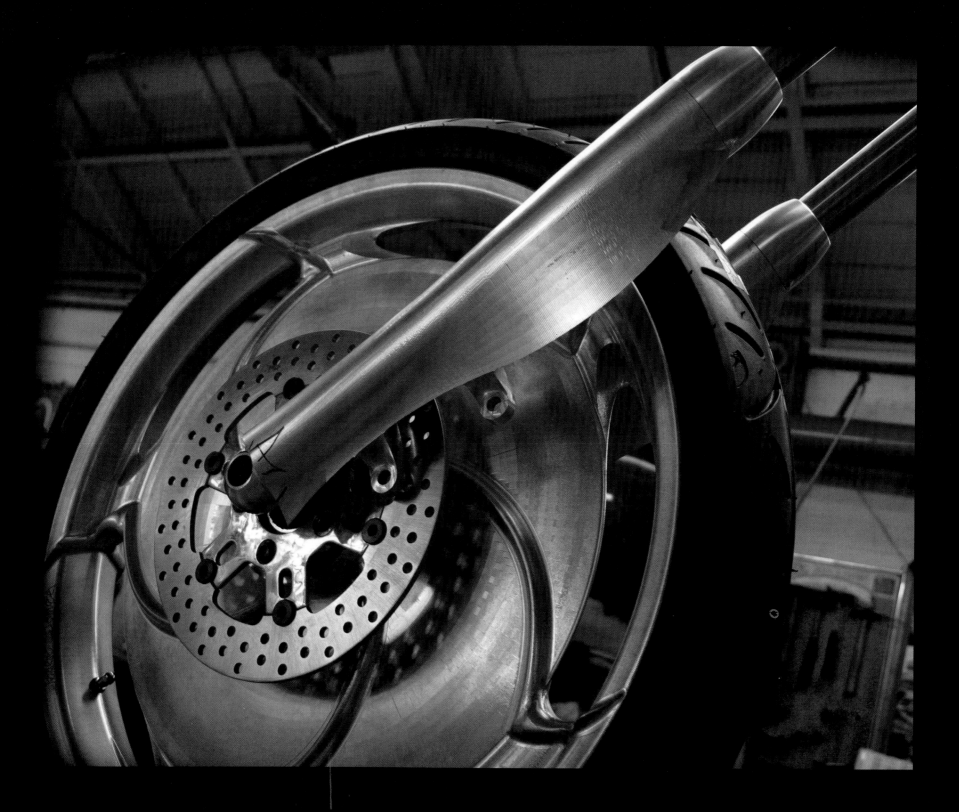

bad
roads.
rigid
frame.
big fun.

the cops and kids laugh through some target practice.

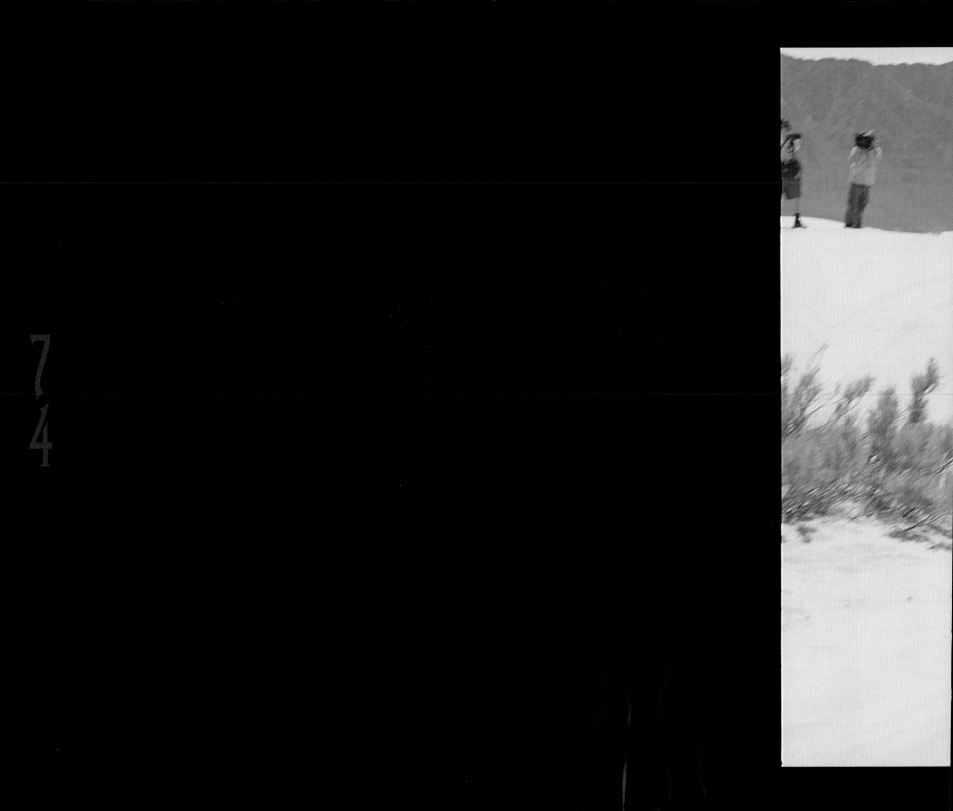

this kind of simplicity is one of the things the two famous gringos came to Mexico to find.

Jesse and Kid cause a commotion in every town

each biker is left to his own thoughts.

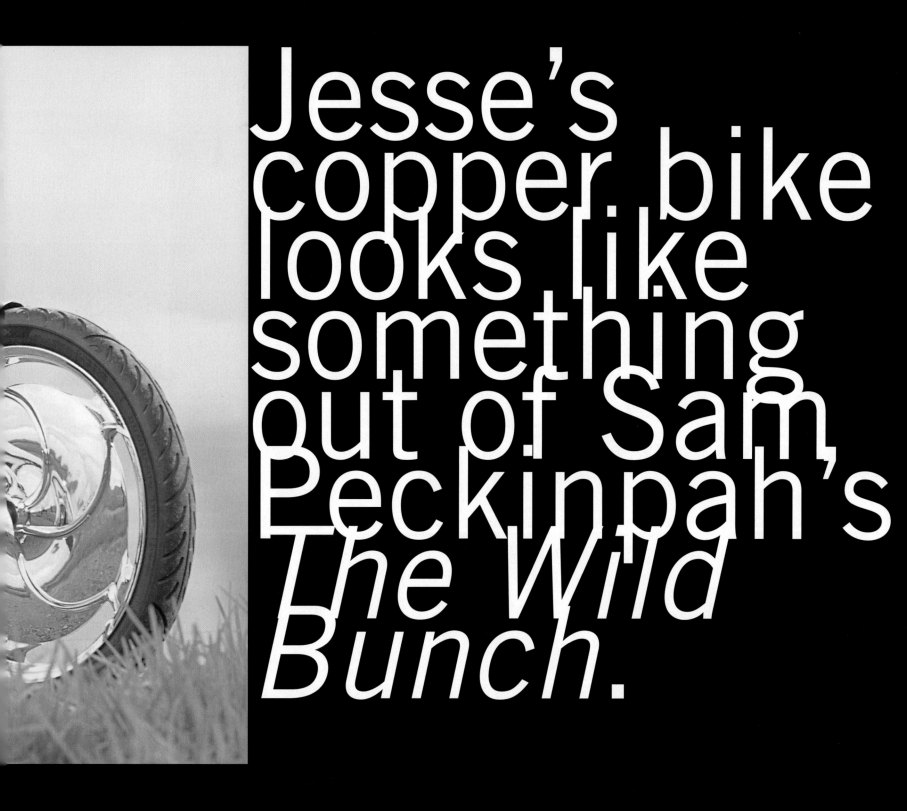

Jesse's copper bike looks like something out of Sam Peckinpah's *The Wild Bunch.*

the way the sun was shining through the clouds—I felt like I was connected.

I'm just
a welder,
a blue-collar,
Dickies-
wearin'
metalfabber.